1970 U.K.

YEARBOOK

ISBN: 9781672282987

This book gives a fascinating and informative insight into life in the United Kingdom in 1970. It includes everything from the most popular music of the year to the cost of a buying a new house. Additionally, there are chapters covering people in high office, the best-selling films of the year and all the main news and events. Want to know which team won the FA Cup or which British personalities were born in 1970? All this and much more awaits you within.

INDEX

FIRST EDITION

1970

January

M	T	W	T	F	S	S
			1	2	3	4
5	6	7	8	9	10	11
12	13	14	15	16	17	18
19	20	21	22	23	24	25
26	27	28	29	30	31	

●:7 ◐:14 ○:22 ◑:30

February

M	T	W	T	F	S	S
						1
2	3	4	5	6	7	8
9	10	11	12	13	14	15
16	17	18	19	20	21	22
23	24	25	26	27	28	

●:6 ◐:13 ○:21

March

M	T	W	T	F	S	S
						1
2	3	4	5	6	7	8
9	10	11	12	13	14	15
16	17	18	19	20	21	22
23	24	25	26	27	28	29
30	31					

◑:1 ●:7 ◐:14 ○:23 ◑:30

April

M	T	W	T	F	S	S
		1	2	3	4	5
6	7	8	9	10	11	12
13	14	15	16	17	18	19
20	21	22	23	24	25	26
27	28	29	30			

●:6 ◐:13 ○:21 ◑:28

May

M	T	W	T	F	S	S
				1	2	3
4	5	6	7	8	9	10
11	12	13	14	15	16	17
18	19	20	21	22	23	24
25	26	27	28	29	30	31

●:5 ◐:13 ○:21 ◑:27

June

M	T	W	T	F	S	S
1	2	3	4	5	6	7
8	9	10	11	12	13	14
15	16	17	18	19	20	21
22	23	24	25	26	27	28
29	30					

●:4 ◐:12 ○:19 ◑:26

July

M	T	W	T	F	S	S
		1	2	3	4	5
6	7	8	9	10	11	12
13	14	15	16	17	18	19
20	21	22	23	24	25	26
27	28	29	30	31		

●:3 ◐:11 ○:18 ◑:25

August

M	T	W	T	F	S	S
					1	2
3	4	5	6	7	8	9
10	11	12	13	14	15	16
17	18	19	20	21	22	23
24	25	26	27	28	29	30
31						

●:2 ◐:10 ○:17 ◑:23 ●:31

September

M	T	W	T	F	S	S
	1	2	3	4	5	6
7	8	9	10	11	12	13
14	15	16	17	18	19	20
21	22	23	24	25	26	27
28	29	30				

◐:8 ○:15 ◑:22 ●:30

October

M	T	W	T	F	S	S
			1	2	3	4
5	6	7	8	9	10	11
12	13	14	15	16	17	18
19	20	21	22	23	24	25
26	27	28	29	30	31	

◐:8 ○:14 ◑:22 ●:30

November

M	T	W	T	F	S	S
						1
2	3	4	5	6	7	8
9	10	11	12	13	14	15
16	17	18	19	20	21	22
23	24	25	26	27	28	29
30						

◐:6 ○:13 ◑:21 ●:28

December

M	T	W	T	F	S	S
	1	2	3	4	5	6
7	8	9	10	11	12	13
14	15	16	17	18	19	20
21	22	23	24	25	26	27
28	29	30	31			

◐:5 ○:12 ◑:20 ●:28

PEOPLE IN HIGH OFFICE

Monarch - Queen Elizabeth II
Reign: 6th February 1952 - Present
Predecessor: King George VI
Heir Apparent: Charles, Prince of Wales

United Kingdom - Prime Ministers

Harold Wilson
Labour Party
16th October 1964 - 19th June 1970

Edward Heath
Conservative Party
19th June 1970 - 4th March 1974

New Zealand

Ireland

United States

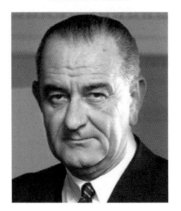

Prime Minister
Keith Holyoake
12th December 1960 -
7th February 1972

Taoiseach
Jack Lynch
10th November 1966 -
14th March 1973

President
Richard Nixon
20th January 1969 -
9th August 1974

 Australia

Prime Minister
John Gorton (1968-1971)

 Brazil

President
Emílio Garrastazú Médici (1969-1974)

 Canada

Prime Minister
Pierre Trudeau (1968-1979)

 China

Communist Party Leader
Mao Zedong (1935-1976)

 France

President
Georges Pompidou (1969-1974)

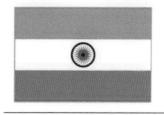 India

Prime Minister
Indira Gandhi (1966-1977)

 Israel

Prime Minister
Golda Meir (1969-1974)

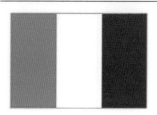 Italy

Prime Minister
Mariano Rumor (1968-1970)
Emilio Colombo (1970-1972)

 Japan

Prime Minister
Eisaku Satō (1964-1972)

 Mexico

President
Gustavo Díaz Ordaz (1964-1970)
Luis Echeverría Álvarez (1970-1976)

 Pakistan

President
Yahya Khan (1969-1971)

 South Africa

Prime Minister
B. J. Vorster (1966-1978)

 Soviet Union

Communist Party Leader
Leonid Brezhnev (1964-1982)

 Spain

Prime Minister
Francisco Franco (1938-1973)

 Turkey

Prime Minister
Süleyman Demirel (1965-1971)

 West Germany

Chancellor
Willy Brandt (1969-1974)

BRITISH NEWS & EVENTS

JAN

1st	The age of majority for most legal purposes is reduced from 21 to 18 under terms of the Family Law Reform Act 1969.
1st	The half-crown coin, first struck in gold in 1526 during the reign of King Henry VIII, ceases to be legal tender; the half crown was equivalent to two shilling and sixpence, or 12½p today.
1st	The National Westminster Bank begins trading following merger of National Provincial Bank and Westminster Bank. *Fun facts: As of 2019 NatWest has over 960 branches, 3,400 cash machines and more than 7.5 million personal customers.*
18th	The 12-foot high grave of Karl Marx is vandalised by explosives at Highgate Cemetery in London.
21st	The Fraserburgh life-boat Duchess of Kent, on service to the Danish fishing vessel Opal, capsizes with the loss of five of the six crew.

22nd January: The first Boeing 747 Jumbo Jet enters service on Pan Am's New York to London route. The 350-ton aircraft's first 324 fare paying passengers land at Heathrow Airport at 2.14pm after a 6.5-hour flight, 7 hours late due to technical problems. *Fun facts: A year after its launch nearly 100 jumbo jets, operated by 17 different airlines, are carrying seven million passengers around the globe.*

26th	Rolling Stones frontman Mick Jagger is fined £200 for possession of cannabis.

Chrysler launches its new Hillman Avenger small family car which is to be built at the Ryton plant near Coventry. *Fun facts: The Avenger was the first and last car to be developed by Rootes (after the Chrysler takeover in 1967) and was built to compete with the likes of the Ford Escort and Vauxhall Viva.*

13th | A demonstration at the Garden House Hotel in Cambridge, by university students against the Greek military junta, leads to police intervention; eight students later receive custodial sentences for their part in the affair.

13th February: The rock band Black Sabbath, formed in Birmingham in 1968, release their self-titled debut album in the U.K. *Follow up: Despite being panned by some critics the album sells in substantial numbers and is eventually certified platinum in both U.K. and the U.S. It is also credited as the first major album in the heavy metal genre. Fun facts: To date Black Sabbath have sold over 70 million records worldwide. They were inducted into the U.K. Music Hall of Fame in 2005, and the Rock and Roll Hall of Fame in 2006. They have also won two Grammy Awards. Photo from left to right: Geezer Butler, Tony Iommi, Bill Ward and Ozzy Osbourne.*

14th | The Who's iconic album Live at Leeds is recorded as a follow up to their 1969 rock opera Tommy; Live at Leeds has been cited by several music critics as the best live rock recording of all time.

17th | Author David Irving is ordered to pay £40,000 libel damages to Captain John Broome over his book, The Destruction of Convoy PQ17. In it he blames the escort group commander Jack Broome for the catastrophic losses of the convoy; the book is withdrawn from circulation.

19th | It is announced that Prince Charles is to join the Royal Navy. He will receive a weekly wage of £15.10s.9d, and is to be known to his mates as Mr Midshipman, His Royal Highness Prince Charles, the Prince of Wales.

FEB

27th	The first National Women's Liberation Conference is held at Ruskin College, Oxford, between the 27th February and 1st March. More than 600 women attend debating a wide variety of issues affecting women. The first four Women's Liberation Movement demands discussed were: 1. Equal pay, 2. Equal educational and job opportunities, 3. Free contraception and abortion on demand, 4. Free 24-hour nurseries.

MAR

2nd	Rhodesian Prime Minister Ian Smith declares Rhodesia a republic. The announcement comes 4½ years after it issued a Unilateral Declaration of Independence from the U.K. (11th November 1965).
6th	The Government announce an indefinite ban on the importation of domestic pets following the death from rabies of a dog called Sessan in Newmarket.
13th	The Bridgwater by-election becomes the first election in which eighteen-year-olds are entitled to vote. Thirty-six-year-old Tom King of the Conservative Party is elected by 10,915 votes, the largest in the constituency for 50 years.
17th	Martin Peters (who scored for England in their 1966 World Cup final win) becomes the nation's first £200,000 footballer with a transfer from West Ham United to Tottenham Hotspur.
26th	The Police (Northern Ireland) Act becomes law. Its aim is to completely reorganise the Royal Ulster Constabulary (RUC), both modernising the force and bringing it into line with the other police forces in the U.K. The act also provides for the disarmament of the RUC and the establishment of an RUC reserve force.
29th	Manchester City win the 10th European Cup Winner's Cup 2-1 in Vienna, Austria, against Górnik Zabrze of Poland.
31st	Following an Orange Order march intense riots erupt on the Springfield Road in Belfast, Northern Ireland. The violence lasts for three days with the army making heavy use of CS gas canisters and grenades in a largely unsuccessful attempt to break up the crowds. Thirty-eight soldiers are injured together with an unknown number of civilians.

APR

6th	PM, presented by William Hardcastle and Derek Cooper, is broadcast for the first time on BBC Radio 4. *Fun fact: PM made history for being the first radio news programme to feature its own theme tune.*
10th	Paul McCartney announces that he is leaving the Beatles; John Lennon had already privately informed his bandmates in September 1969 that he was leaving the band.
16th	Dr. Ian Paisley, standing on behalf of the Protestant Unionist Party in a by-election to the Northern Ireland Parliament, wins the Bannside seat formerly held by Prime Minister Terence O'Neill. *Follow up: On the 30th September 1971 Paisley founded the Democratic Unionist Party (DUP), a party he would go on to lead for almost forty years.*
20th	Englishman Ron Hill wins the 74th Boston Marathon in a time of 2h 10m 30s. *Fun fact: The Boston Marathon is the world's oldest annual marathon.*

MAY

6th	Dutch team Feyenoord beats Celtic 2-1 to win the European Cup Final. The match was played at the San Siro stadium in Milan in front of 53,187 fans.
8th	The Beatles release Let It Be, their 12th and final studio album. *Fun facts: The album was released in tandem with the motion picture of the same name. Following its release, the Beatles collectively won the 1970 Academy Award for Best Original Song Score.*
22nd	A tour by the all-white South African cricket team is called off after an emergency meeting at Lord's cricket headquarters in London. The decision was made after a request was made by the government to cancel the tour.
24th	The Britannia Bridge, carrying a railway across the Menai Strait between the island of Anglesey and mainland Wales, is badly damaged by fire. *Follow up: Following an investigation it was determined that the damage caused by the fire was so extensive that the bridge would need to be rebuilt. The new the structure was to support not one, but two decks, and function as a combined road-and-rail bridge.*
25th	Bobby Moore, captain of the England national football team, is charged and placed under house arrest at the home of a local football official in Bogotá, Colombia, on suspicion of stealing a $1,500 emerald bracelet. *Follow up: On the 28th May Judge Pedro Dorado decided that there was no evidence to warrant jailing Moore and he was freed, with conditions, so that he could play at the World Cup in Mexico.*
27th	Don Whillans and Dougal Haston, members of a British expedition led by Sir Chris Bonington, become the first to climb the south face of the 26,000-foot Himalayan massif Annapurna in north-central Nepal.
29th	The Law Reform (Miscellaneous Provisions) Act abolishes actions for breach of promise and the right to claim damages for adultery.

JUN

1st	Prime Minister Harold Wilson is hit in the face with an egg thrown at close range by Richard Ware, a Young Conservative demonstrator.

2nd June: In Pembrokeshire a 230-foot (70-metre) cantilever, being used to put one of the 150-tonne sections of the Cleddau Bridge into position, collapses on the south side of the estuary. Four workers die and five are injured. An inquiry into the collapse leads to the introduction of new standards for box girder bridges.

JUN

4th	The British protectorate Tonga acquires its independence and becomes a sovereign nation.
7th	The Who become the first act to perform rock music (their rock opera Tommy) at the Metropolitan Opera House in New York.
13th	Actor Laurence Olivier is made a life peer in the Queen's Birthday Honours list for his services to the theatre. *Fun facts: Olivier was the first actor to be made a lord and was subsequently created Baron Olivier, of Brighton in the County of Sussex.*
14th	England's defence of the FIFA World Cup ends when they lose 3-2 to West Germany at their quarter final match in Mexico.
17th	The bodies of two children are found buried in shallow graves in a copse of trees at the edge of Epping Forest. They are believed to be those of Susan Blatchford (aged 11) and Gary Hanlon (aged 12) who were last seen alive near their homes in North London on the 31st March. *Follow up: Ronald Jebson, already serving life for murdering 8-year-old Rosemary Papper in 1974, was convicted for their murders on the 9th May 2000 at the Old Bailey.*
17th	British Leyland create a niche in the four-wheel drive market by launching its luxury Range Rover at Blue Hills Mine, St. Agnes, Cornwall. Marketed as a more upmarket urban alternative to the utilitarian Land Rover that had been in production since 1948, it went up for sale with a price tag of £1,998 including tax.
17th	David Storey's play, Home, starring John Gielgud, Ralph Richardson, Dandy Nichols and Mona Washbourne, premieres at the Royal Court Theatre in London.
18th	The 1970 general election is held with opinion polls pointing towards a third consecutive victory for the Labour Government led by Harold Wilson. *Fun fact: This is the first general election in which 18-year-olds are eligible vote after the passage of the Representation of the People Act in 1969.*
19th	The general election results are announced and Edward Heath's Conservative Party, along with the Ulster Unionist Party, secure a majority of 31 seats to oust the Labour government of Harold Wilson after nearly six years in power. The surprise result sees amongst its new Members of Parliament Conservatives Kenneth Clarke, Norman Tebbit John Gummer and Alan Haselhurst, and for Labour Neil Kinnock, John Smith, John Prescott and Dennis Skinner.
21st	British golfer Tony Jacklin wins the U.S. Open at Hazeltine National Golf Club in Chaska, Minnesota. His seven-stroke victory sees him take home $30,000 and the second of his two major championships.
26th	Riots break out in Londonderry after the arrest of Mid-Ulster MP Bernadette Devlin (for her part in the Bogside riots in 1969). *Follow up: Devlin was released from prison on the 21st October having served four months of a six-month sentence.*

JUL

1st	After a visit to Northern Ireland Home Secretary Reginald Maudling is reported as saying: "For God's sake bring me a large Scotch. What a bloody awful country".

3rd July: The Falls Curfew (3rd - 5th July): A British Army raid in the Falls district of Belfast develops into a riot between soldiers and residents, and then gun battles between soldiers and the Irish Republican Army. This leads to the Army sealing off the area, imposing a 36-hour curfew and raiding hundreds of homes under the cover of CS gas. During the operation large quantities of weapons and ammunition were captured. Four civilians were killed by the British Army and at least 78 people were wounded, 337 were arrested. Eighteen soldiers were also wounded. On the 5th July the curfew was brought to an end when thousands of women and children from Andersonstown marched into the curfew zone with food and other supplies for the locals. *Follow up: The Falls Curfew was a turning point in the Troubles. It is seen as having turned many Catholics/Irish nationalists against the British Army and having boosted support for the IRA. Photo: 4th July 1970: The British Army take up defensive positions on the Falls Road.*

3rd	Dan-Air Flight 1903: A de Havilland Comet 4 aircraft carrying a group of holidaymakers from Manchester to Barcelona crashes into the wooded slopes of the Serralada del Montseny in Catalonia, Spain. The crash results in the deaths of all 112 on board and is the deadliest aviation accident of 1970.
8th	Roy Jenkins defeats future Labour Leader Michael Foot and former Leader of the Commons Fred Peart to become Deputy Leader of the Labour Party.
14th	Five speedway riders die in Lokeren, Belgium when a minibus carrying members of the West Ham speedway team crashes into two lorries and a petrol tanker after a brief tour.
16th	Major industrial action by 47,000 dockers in the U.K. raises fears of food shortages and leads to a proclamation of a state of emergency by the Queen.

JUL

16th	The Commonwealth Games opening ceremony takes place in Edinburgh; it is the first time the event has ever been held in Scotland.
23rd	Shouts of "Belfast! See how you like it!" are heard as two CS gas canisters are thrown by a demonstrator into the chamber of the House of Commons. Police later charge 26-year-old labourer James Anthony Roche with possessing a prohibited weapon under the Firearms Act of 1968.
30th	After a largely peaceful strike the dock strike is settled. Union delegates vote by 51 to 31 to accept an average 7% increase in dockers' wages.
31st	Black Tot Day: The last officially sanctioned rum ration is issued by the Royal Navy to its sailors.

AUG

2nd	Rubber bullets are used for the first time in Northern Ireland.
20th	The moderate Social Democratic and Labour Party is established in Northern Ireland.

26th August: The third Isle of Wight Festival (26th - 31st August) attracts over 600,000 pop music fans and includes appearances by Jimi Hendrix, Chicago, The Doors, Lighthouse, The Moody Blues, The Who, Miles Davis, Joan Baez, Joni Mitchell, Jethro Tull, Sly and the Family Stone, Emerson, Lake & Palmer, and Free. Held at Afton Down, an area on the western side of the Isle of Wight, the festival is widely acknowledged as the largest musical event of its time, breaking Woodstock's record of 400,000 attendees.

AUG

27th | The Royal Shakespeare Company's revolutionary production of A Midsummer Night's Dream, directed by Peter Brook, opens at Stratford-upon-Avon.

SEP

| The album of the rock opera Jesus Christ Superstar, by Andrew Lloyd Webber and Tim Rice, is released. This musical dramatisation of the last week of the life of Jesus Christ was originally banned by the BBC on grounds of being "sacrilegious"; it went on to sell over 7 million copies worldwide.

9th | BOAC Flight 775 is hijacked after taking off from Bahrain. The hijacking was the work of a PFLP (Popular Front for the Liberation of Palestine) sympathiser who wanted to influence the British government to free Leila Khaled.

18th | American rock star Jimi Hendrix, 27, dies from a suspected drug-induced heart attack at the Samarkand Hotel in Notting Hill, London. *Follow up: The post-mortem examination concluded that Hendrix aspirated on his own vomit and died of asphyxia while intoxicated with barbiturates. At the inquest, the coroner, finding no evidence of suicide and lacking sufficient evidence of the circumstances, recorded an open verdict.*

19th | The first Glastonbury Festival (then named the Pilton Pop, Blues & Folk Festival) is held at Worthy Farm in Pilton, Somerset. Organised by farmer Michael Eavis, 1,500 paid £1 each to watch the likes of Tyrannosaurus Rex, Quintessence, Stackridge, and Al Stewart.

OCT

2nd | Pink Floyd release their fifth studio album Atom Heart Mother; it becomes their first album to reach No.1 in the UK. *Fun facts: The cover, showing a Holstein-Friesian cow standing in a pasture, was designed by Hipgnosis and was the first not feature the band's name or include any photograph of the band.*

3rd October: Tony Densham averages 207.6mph over a flying kilometre to set a British land speed record at Elvington near York. *Fun facts: The record broke the 174.88mph record set 43 years earlier by Sir Malcolm Campbell. Photo: Tony Densham (obscured by smoke) driving the record setting Ford-powered "Commuter" dragster.*

OCT

5th	BBC Radio 4 first broadcasts its consumer affairs magazine programme You and Yours; it is still running as of 2019.
7th	British Petroleum announce they had struck oil 110 miles (180km) east of Aberdeen in the Long Forties area of the North Sea. *Fun facts: The Forties Oil Field is the largest oil field in the U.K. sector of the North Sea. Production from the field peaked in 1979 at 500 thousand barrels per day (79 thousand cubic metres per day), well above early predictions.*
13th	The Gay Liberation Front has its first meeting in the basement of the London School of Economics.
15th	The Department of the Environment is created as a combination of the Ministry of Housing and Local Government, the Ministry of Transport, and the Ministry of Public Building and Works.
15th	The Thames sailing barge Cambria, the last vessel trading under sail alone in British waters, loads her last freight at Tilbury (100 tons of cattle cake).
19th	The government creates the Department of Trade and Industry; the DTI was eventually replaced on the 28th June 2007 with the Department for Business, Enterprise and Regulatory Reform, and the Department for Innovation, Universities and Skills.
23rd	The Mark III Ford Cortina goes on sale. At launch a full range of models are offered including two-door and estate variants. Unlike previous models, this Cortina was developed as a Ford Europe model sharing the floor-pan with the German Ford Taunus.
25th	The canonisation of the Forty Martyrs of England and Wales by Pope Paul VI takes place in Rome.

NOV

8th	The British comedy television series The Goodies, starring Tim Brooke-Taylor, Graeme Garden and Bill Oddie, debuts on BBC Two.
17th	The Sun newspaper celebrates its first anniversary as a tabloid newspaper by publishing a nude photograph of 22-year-old Singapore born model Stephanie Khan on page 3. Khan (mis-spelt Rahn in the newspaper) becomes the very first Page Three girl.
20th	The Miss World 1970 beauty pageant, hosted by Bob Hope at the Royal Albert Hall in London, sees Jennifer Hosten from Grenada crowned Miss World. The event was marked by controversy in the days beforehand, during the contest itself, and afterwards.
22nd	The ten-shilling note, first introduced in 1928, ceases to be legal tender. It had been replaced by a new 50 pence coin in 1969 as part of the process of decimalisation.
29th	England batsman Colin Cowdrey becomes Test Cricket's leading run scorer at the 1st Test against Australia in Brisbane; he passes countryman Wally Hammond's world Test-record aggregate of 7,249 runs.

DEC

31st	Paul McCartney files a lawsuit against the other members of The Beatles to dissolve their partnership, effectively ending the band.

75 WORLDWIDE NEWS & EVENTS

1. 5th January: An earthquake with a moment magnitude of 7.1 shakes Tonghai County in Yunnan province, China. With a maximum Mercalli intensity of X (extreme) the tremor is felt over an area of 3,390 sq mi (8,781 km^2). Estimates put the number of deaths caused by the quake at between 10,000 and 15,000.

2. 15th January: After a 32-month fight for independence Biafran forces (under Philip Effiong) surrender to the Nigerian Federal Military Government (FMG) ending the Nigerian Civil War.

3. 16th January: Colonel Muammar Gaddafi is proclaimed premier of Libya.

4. 23rd January: Australia's first amateur radio satellite Oscar 5, built by students at the University of Melbourne, is launched from Vandenberg Air Force Base in the U.S state of California.

5. 31st January: I Want You Back becomes the Jackson 5's first Billboard No.1 Hot 100 single in America. *Fun facts: The song eventually goes on to sell six million copies worldwide and in 1999 is inducted into the Grammy Hall of Fame.*

6. 1st February: A train crash at Benavidez near Buenos Aires, Argentina, kills 236 and injures 500. It is Argentina's (and South America's) worst-ever rail disaster.

7. 10th February: An avalanche at the fashionable Val d'Isere ski resort in the French Alps crashes into a hotel killing 42 and injuring 60.

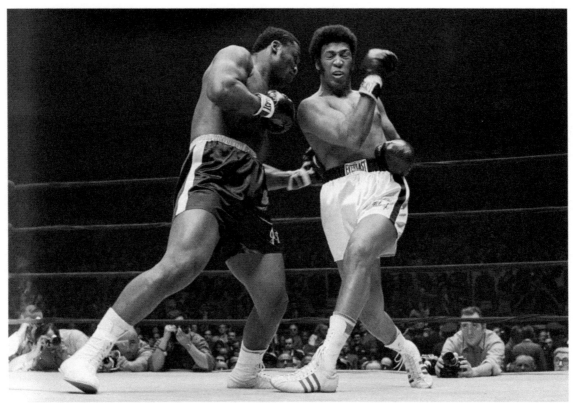

8. 16th February: Joe Frazier wins the WBA and vacant WBC world heavyweight boxing titles with a TKO over Jimmy Ellis; Ellis's trainer Angelo Dundee would not let him come out for the 5th round following two 4th round knockdowns (the first knockdowns of Ellis's career). *Photo: Joe Frazier (left) and Jimmy Ellis slug it out for the undisputed heavyweight title at Madison Square Garden in New York.*

9. | 19th February: Shares in Australian nickel mining company Poseidon NL, which had stood at $0.80 five months earlier, peak at around $280 before the speculative bubble bursts.

10. | 20th February: Construction begins on the Boğaziçi Bridge crossing the Bosphorus in Istanbul, Turkey. *Fun fact: The bridge opens on the 30th October 1973 and is the first modern bridge connecting Europe and Asia.*

11. | 22nd February: Guyana officially becomes a Republic within the Commonwealth of Nations; Guyana gained its independence from the United Kingdom on the 26th May 1966.

12. | 4th March: All 57 men aboard the French submarine Eurydice (S644) are killed when the vessel explodes off Cape Camarat in the Mediterranean Sea.

13. | 5th March: The Nuclear Non-Proliferation Treaty goes into effect after ratification by 43 nations.

14. | 15th March: The Expo '70 World's Fair opens in Suita, Osaka, Japan. The theme of the Expo is "Progress and Harmony for Mankind".

15. | 19th March: The leaders of East and West Germany meet at a summit for the first time since Germany's division into two republics. West German Chancellor Willy Brandt is greeted by cheering East German crowds as he arrives in Erfurt for the summit with his counterpart, East German Ministerpräsident Willi Stoph.

16. | 21st March: The first Earth Day proclamation is issued by San Francisco Mayor Joseph Alioto. *Fun fact: American peace activist John McConnell first introduced the idea of a global holiday called 'Earth Day' at the 1969 UNESCO Conference on the Environment.*

17. 21st March: All Kinds of Everything, sung by 18-year-old schoolgirl Dana (born Rosemary Brown), wins the 15th Eurovision Song Contest for Ireland in Amsterdam; Mary Hopkin comes in second for the United Kingdom singing "Knock, Knock Who's There?".

18. | 31st March: Japan Airlines Flight 351, carrying 122 passengers and 7 crew from Tokyo to Fukuoka, is hijacked by 9 members of the Japanese Red Army armed with samurai swords and pipe bombs. All passengers and crew are eventually freed.

19. | 4th April: A group of special KGB agents in Magdeburg, East Germany, open the grave of Adolf Hitler, Eva Braun, Joseph Goebbels, Magda Goebbels and the Goebbels children. The remains are burnt on a bonfire outside the town of Shoenebeck, 11 kilometres away from Magdeburg, then ground into ashes, collected and thrown into the Biederitz River.

20.	7th April: The 42nd Academy Awards are presented at the Dorothy Chandler Pavilion in Los Angeles, California, honouring the best in film for 1969. The winners include Midnight Cowboy for Best Picture, and John Wayne and Maggie Smith for Best Actor and Actress.
21.	8th April: A huge gas explosion at a subway construction site in Osaka, Japan, kills 79, injures 420, and destroys 495 houses and buildings.
22.	8th April: Israeli Air Force F-4 Phantom II fighter bombers kill 46 children at an elementary school in the Egyptian village of Bahr el-Baqar. The school, mistakenly identified as an Egyptian military installation by Israel, was hit by five bombs and two air-to-ground missiles.

23. 11th April: Apollo 13, carrying Jim Lovell, Fred Haise and Jack Swigert, is launched from the Kennedy Space Center in Florida toward the Moon. It is the seventh crewed mission of the Apollo space program and the third intended to land on the Moon. Two days into the mission the lunar landing is aborted after an oxygen tank explodes in the service module. The crew instead loop around the Moon and, despite great hardship, make it safely back to Earth on the 17th April. *Pictured: The crew of Apollo 13 with President Richard Nixon.*

24.	16th April: A landslide kills 71 after thousands of tons of mud crash onto the boys' wing of a tuberculosis sanatorium in the French Alps.
25.	19th April: The 24th Annual Tony Awards are broadcast on NBC television from the Mark Hellinger Theatre in New York City. Hosted by Julie Andrews, Shirley MacLaine and Walter Matthau, the winners include Borstal Boy (best play) and Applause (best musical).
26.	21st April: Leonard Casley attempts to secede from Australia, declaring his farm to be an independent country; the new Hutt River Province is not though recognised as a country by the Australian Government or any other national government. *Fun facts: Today the Principality of Hutt River is a regional tourist attraction issuing its own currency, stamps and passports (none of which are officially recognised by any other nation).*
27.	24th April: China's first satellite, the 173kg Dong Fang Hong 1, is launched into oribit. In addition to performing tests of satellite technology, and taking readings of the ionosphere and atmosphere, it also carries a radio transmitter broadcasting the country's national anthem.
28.	26th April: The World Intellectual Property Organization (WIPO) is formerly created.

29. 29th April: The U.S. invades Cambodia and begins its campaign to try to defeat approximately 40,000 troops of the People's Army of Vietnam (PAVN) and the Viet Cong (VC) in the eastern border regions of Cambodia.

30. 6th May: Future Taoiseach Charles Haughey and Neil Blaney are dismissed as members of the Irish Government over accusations of their involvement in a plot to import arms for use by the Provisional IRA in Northern Ireland.

31. 14th May: Ulrike Meinhof helps Andreas Baader escape from custody and create the Red Army Faction (also known as the Baader–Meinhof Gang).

32. 16th May: The movie M*A*S*H, directed by Robert Altman, wins the Palme d'Or at the 23rd Cannes Film Festival.

33. 17th May: Norwegian adventurer Thor Heyerdahl and a multinational crew set sail from Morocco on a papyrus boat called Ra II. Sailing with the Canary Current he reaches Barbados after 57 days, thus demonstrating that ancient mariners could have dealt with trans-Atlantic voyages. *Fun facts: Heyerdahl first became well known for his Kon-Tiki expedition in 1947, sailing 5,000 miles (8,000km) across the Pacific Ocean in a hand-built raft from South America to the Tuamotu Islands. That expedition was designed to demonstrate that ancient peoples could have made long sea voyages and created contacts between separate cultures. Notes: The Ra II is now in the Kon-Tiki Museum in Oslo, Norway. Photos: Ra II on the 17th May 1970 at the fishing port of Safi in Morocco / Thor Heyerdahl.*

34. 26th May: The Soviet Tupolev Tu-144 becomes the first commercial supersonic transport aircraft to exceed Mach 2.

35. 31st May: A 7.9Mw earthquake shakes the Peruvian regions of Ancash and La Libertad. Combined with a resultant landslide it is the most catastrophic natural disaster in the history of Peru. The number of people killed is estimated to be between 66,794 and 70,000; 50,000 are injured.

36. 31st May: The 9th FIFA World Cup begins in Mexico (it is the first time the tournament has been staged outside Europe and South America).

37. 1st June: Soyuz 9 is launched in the Soviet Union. *Fun fact: The two-man crew of Andrian Nikolayev and Vitali Sevastyanov break the 5-year-old space endurance record held by the crew of NASA's Gemini 7, spending nearly 18-days in space.*

38. 19th June: The Patent Cooperation Treaty is signed into international law providing a unified procedure for filing patent applications to protect inventions.

39. | 21st June: Brazil defeats Italy 4-1 to win the FIFA World Cup in front of 107,412 fans in Mexico City. *Fun fact: The win sees Brazil and Pelé become first team and player to win the World Cup 3 times.*

40. | 22nd June: Twenty-eight-year-old twister Chubby Checker (real name Ernest Evans) and three members of his band are arrested for marijuana possession while returning to the U.S. after an appearance in Canada. *Follow up: Charges against Checker were dropped on the 22nd July but the three other band members were each fined $250 after admitting possession of drugs.*

41. | 3rd July: Dan-Air Flight 1903 (a de Havilland Comet) crashes into the wooded slopes of the Serralada del Montseny near Arbúcies (Girona), Catalonia, Spain. All 112 on board are killed.

42. 3rd July: The second Atlanta International Pop Festival is held in Byron, Georgia. Promoted as "three days of peace, love and music", tickets for the festival were priced at $14. It became a free event when the promoters threw open the gates after large crowds outside began chanting, "Free, free, free. Music belongs to the people", and threatened to overwhelm the security crew the promoters had hired. Over thirty acts performed on the main stage during the course of the event in front of crowds estimated to have been between 150,000 and 600,000. *Follow up: Georgia's colourful governor, Lester Maddox, who had tried repeatedly to prevent the festival from taking place, vowed that he would do whatever it took to block any similar event in the future - A third Atlanta Pop Festival never took place! Fun fact: Jimi Hendrix performed his unique rendition of the "Star-Spangled Banner", at midnight on the 4th July, to the largest American audience of his career.*

43.	5th July: Air Canada Flight 621 (a Douglas DC-8) crashes at Toronto International Airport in Ontario, Canada. All 109 passengers and crew are killed.
44.	21st July: The Aswan High Dam, built across the Nile in Aswan, Egypt, is completed.
45.	23rd July: Said bin Taimur, Sultan of Muscat and Oman, is deposed in a palace coup by his son, Qaboos. The coup is supported by the British and is sanctioned by Prime Minister Harold Wilson.
46.	17th August: The Soviet probe Venera 7 is launched toward Venus. *Follow up: When it landed on the Venusian surface (15th December 1970) it became the first spacecraft to soft land on another planet and first to transmit data from there back to Earth.*
47.	25th August: Elton John makes his U.S. debut in front of 300 people at the Troubadour in Los Angeles.
48.	5th September: Austrian Formula One driver Jochen Rindt is killed in qualifying for the Italian Grand Prix. *Follow up: Rindt had already won five of the first nine races of the F1 season which was enough for him to be named the Formula One World Champion. He is the only driver to have been posthumously awarded the title.*
49.	9th September: Elvis Presley appears in front of 13,000 fans at the Veterans Memorial Coliseum in Phoenix, Arizona. It is the start of his first concert tour since October 1957.
50.	12th September: The Soviet spacecraft Luna 16 is launched; it becomes the first robotic probe to land on the Moon and return a sample of lunar soil to Earth (24th September).
51.	19th September: Kostas Georgakis, a Greek student of geology, sets himself ablaze in Matteotti Square in Genoa, Italy, as a protest against the dictatorial regime of Greece's Georgios Papadopoulos.
52.	20th September: Doors front man Jim Morrison is found guilty of "open profanity and indecent exposure" after allegedly exposing himself at a concert in Miami in 1969.
53.	27th September: U.S. President Richard Nixon begins a tour of Europe, visiting Italy, Yugoslavia, Spain, the United Kingdom and Ireland.
54.	27th September: Pope Paul VI names Saint Teresa of Ávila as the first female Doctor of the Church in recognition of her centuries-long spiritual legacy to Catholicism.
55.	4th October: In Los Angeles, California, 27-year-old rock musician Janis Joplin dies in her hotel room from a heroin overdose.
56.	5th October: The Front de libération du Québec (FLQ) kidnaps British diplomat James Cross in Montreal and demands the release of all its imprisoned members. The next day the Canadian government announces it will not meet the demand, beginning the October Crisis. *Follow up: Cross is released after 62 days in return for the Canadian Government granting 5 FLQ terrorists safe passage to Cuba.*
57.	9th October: The Khmer Republic is proclaimed in Cambodia.
58.	10th October: Fiji gains its independence from the United Kingdom.
59.	15th October: In the United Arab Republic (Egypt) a referendum supports Anwar Sadat to become president with 90% of the vote - he ran unopposed.
60.	15th October: Aeroflot Flight 244 is hijacked by Lithuanian Pranas Brazinskas and his 13-year-old son Algirdas. The flight is diverted to Turkey and is the first known successful airline hijacking in the Soviet Union.
61.	16th October: Canada's Prime Minister Pierre Trudeau invokes the War Measures Act as a response to the October Crisis, the only peacetime use of the War Measures Act in Canadian history.

62.	21st October: American agronomist Norman Ernest Borlaug is awarded the Nobel Peace Prize for his work in food production and hunger alleviation.
63.	23rd October: American motorsport driver Gary Gabelich sets the world land speed record over a flying mile (622.407mph) in a rocket-powered car. The feat was achieved at the Bonneville Salt Flats near Wendover, Utah, in a car called Blue Flame.
64.	1st November: A major blaze at Club Cinq-Sept, a nightclub just outside Saint-Laurent-du-Pont, Isère in south-eastern France, kills 146.
65.	3rd - 13th November: Bhola cyclone: A 115mph (185km/h) tropical cyclone hits the densely populated Ganges Delta region of East Pakistan (now Bangladesh), killing an estimated 500,000 people; it remains today the deadliest tropical cyclone ever recorded.
66.	10th November: The Soviet spacecraft Luna 17 is launched. Seven days into its mission it deploys the first remote-controlled robotic rover (Lunokhod 1) onto the surface of the Moon.
67.	17th November: Douglas Engelbart receives a U.S. patent for a computer mouse (described in his application as an X-Y Position Indicator for a Display System).
68.	17th November: Vietnam War: U.S Army officer Lieutenant William Calley goes on trial charged with six specifications of premeditated murder for the deaths of 109 unarmed South Vietnamese civilians in My Lai on the 16th March 1968. *Follow up: On the 29th March 1971 he is convicted murdering 22 and sentenced to life imprisonment and hard labour. Instead of prison he is put under house arrest under orders from President Nixon. He is subsequently released after serving just three and a half years.*
69.	18th November: Joe Frazier knocks out World Light Heavyweight Champion Bob Foster in the second round to retain his heavyweight boxing titles. This match sets up what is billed as the "Fight of the Century" against Muhammad Ali at Madison Square Garden in New York City on the 8th March 1971.
70.	25th November: In Tokyo, author and Tatenokai militia leader Yukio Mishima and his followers take over the headquarters of the Japan Self-Defense Forces in an attempted coup d'état. After Mishima's speech fails to sway public opinion towards his right-wing political beliefs, including restoration of the powers of the Emperor, he commits seppuku (public ritual suicide by disembowelment).
71.	27th November: Pope Paul VI is wounded in chest during a visit to Philippines. The attack is carried out by dagger-wielding Bolivian artist Benjamin Mendoza who is disguised as a priest.
72.	14th - 19th December: After the government of Poland announces a sudden increase in the prices of food and other everyday items, strikes occur across the northern parts of the country. As a result of the strikes, which were put down by the Polish People's Army and the Citizen's Militia, at least 42 people are killed and more than 1,000 wounded.
73.	14th December: The overloaded South Korean ferryboat Namyong Ho capsizes in the Korea Strait killing 323 people.
74.	23rd December: The North Tower of the World Trade Center in New York is topped out at 1,368 feet making it the tallest building in the world. *Fun facts: The twin towers knocked New York City's own Empire State Building (1931, 1,250 feet) off the top of the list of the world's tallest buildings, but lost out in 1974 to Chicago's Sears Tower at 1,451 feet. Since 2009 the Burj Khalifa in Dubai, United Arab Emirates, has been the world's tallest building at a total height of 2,722 ft.*
75.	29th December: Ballon d'Or: Bayern Munich striker Gerd Müller wins the award for best European football player. West Ham United's defender Bobby Moore came in second and Cagliari forward Luigi Riva third.

BIRTHS
U.K. PERSONALITIES
BORN IN 1970

Andrew Murray Burnham
b. 7th January 1970

Labour Party politician who served as the MP for Leigh from 2001 to 2017, and has been the Mayor of Greater Manchester since May 2017. During his time as an MP Burnham served as Secretary of State for Culture, Media and Sport from 2008 to 2009, and Secretary of State for Health from 2009 until 2010. After Labour lost the 2015 general election Burnham launched a campaign to succeed Ed Miliband as leader of the Labour Party but finished a distant second to Jeremy Corbyn.

Timothy James Carrington Foster, MBE
b. 19th January 1970

Rower who won a gold medal at the Sydney 2000 Olympics and was the first Britain to win gold medals at two consecutive World Rowing Junior Championships (1987, 1988). After the Sydney Olympics Foster retired from international rowing, and in July 2001 retired as an active rower completely. In January 2007 he became the head coach of the Swiss national rowing squad and remained in this role until 2012. He now works as a business coach.

Amelia Fiona 'Minnie' Driver
b. 31st January 1970

An English-American actress and singer-songwriter. She was nominated for an Oscar for Best Supporting Actress for her role as Skylar in Good Will Hunting (1997), and for Emmy and Golden Globe Awards for the television series The Riches (2007-2008). On the big screen she has starred in films such as Sleepers (1996), Big Night (1996), The Phantom of the Opera (2004), and Barney's Version (2010). On television she has had leading roles in the American sitcoms About a Boy (2014-2015) and Speechless (2016-2019).

Warwick Ashley Davis
b. 3rd February 1970

Actor, television presenter, writer, director, and producer. His film roles include playing the Ewok 'Wicket' in Star Wars Episode VI: Return of the Jedi (1983), the title characters in Willow (1988) and the Leprechaun film series, and Professor Filius Flitwick and Griphook in the Harry Potter films. On television Davis has starred as a fictionalised version of himself in the sitcom Life's Too Short (2011-2013), and has presented the ITV game shows Celebrity Squares (2014-2015) and Tenable (2016-present).

Simon John Pegg,
b. 14th February 1970

Actor, comedian, screenwriter, and producer who came to public prominence as the co-creator of the Channel 4 sitcom Spaced (1999-2001). He then went on to co-write and star in the Three Flavours Cornetto film trilogy: Shaun of the Dead (2004), Hot Fuzz (2007), and The World's End (2013). Other notable film roles include playing Benji Dunn in the Mission: Impossible film series (2006–present), and Montgomery Scott in Star Trek (2009), Star Trek Into Darkness (2013), and Star Trek Beyond (2016), co-writing the latter.

Rachel Hannah Weisz
b. 7th March 1970

An English-American actress who has been the recipient of an Academy Award, a BAFTA Award, a Golden Globe Award, a Critics' Choice Award, and a Screen Actors Guild Award. She began her acting career in the early 1990s appearing in television series such as Inspector Morse and Scarlet and Black. She made her film debut in Death Machine (1994) and made her Hollywood breakthrough in the blockbuster action films The Mummy (1999), and The Mummy Returns (2001).

Louis Sebastian Theroux
b. 20th May 1970

Documentary filmmaker, journalist and broadcaster who first moved into television as the presenter of offbeat segments on Michael Moore's TV Nation series. He is best known for his documentary series including Louis Theroux's Weird Weekends, When Louis Met..., and several BBC Two specials. Theroux has received two British Academy Television Awards and a Royal Television Society Television Award for his work.

Naomi Elaine Campbell
b. 22nd May 1970

Model, actress, and businesswoman. Discovered at the age of 15 she established herself amongst the most recognisable and in-demand models of the late 1980s and the 1990s, and was one of six models of her generation declared supermodels by the fashion industry and the international press. In addition to her modelling career she has embarked on a number of other ventures, these have included making an R&B pop studio album and making several acting appearances on film and television.

Lucy Benjamin
b. 25th June 1970

Actress born Lucy Jane Baker who is best known for playing Lisa Fowler in the BBC soap opera EastEnders; during her time on EastEnders she was involved in one of the soap's most viewed storylines, Who Shot Phil? (2001). In June 2006 Benjamin appeared on The X Factor: Battle of the Stars and was the outright winner for Simon Cowells over 25's group. In September 2008 she appeared on All Star Family Fortunes, winning £10,000 for her charity Rosie's Rainbow Fund.

Jason Thomas Orange
b. 10th July 1970

Retired singer, songwriter, dancer, musician and actor who started his career as part of the Manchester-based breakdance crew 'Street Machine' in the mid-1980s. Orange is best known as a member of the pop group Take That (1990 to 1996, and again following their reunion in 2005 until 2014). As a member of Take That Orange has had 11 No.1 singles, 7 No.1 albums, and received eight Brit Awards and an Ivor Novello Award for Outstanding Contribution to British Music.

Andi Eleazu Peters
b. 29th July 1970

Television presenter, producer, journalist, voice-over artist, and voice actor currently employed by ITV. He is best known for his roles on the Breakfast TV shows Live & Kicking, GMTV, Good Morning Britain and Lorraine, and for hosting Dancing on Ice: Extra, and The Big Reunion. He also took part in the third series of Celebrity MasterChef (2008) finishing runner-up. On radio Peters has been a regular guest on The Chris Moyles Show, originally on BBC Radio 1 and from 2015 on Radio X.

Christopher Edward Nolan, CBE
b. 30th July 1970

Film director, screenwriter and producer who holds both British and American citizenship. He made his directorial debut with Following (1998) and went on to find popular and critical success with The Dark Knight Trilogy (2005-2012), Inception (2010), Interstellar (2014), and Dunkirk (2017). His films have to date grossed over US$4.7 billion worldwide and garnered a total of 34 Academy Award nominations, including ten wins. Nolan was appointed a CBE in the 2019 New Year Honours for his services to film.

Alan Shearer, CBE, DL
b. 13th August 1970

Retired footballer who played as a striker for Southampton, Blackburn Rovers and Newcastle United. Shearer scored 283 league goals in his career (all in the first tier of English football), including a record 260 in the Premier League. He also played 63 times for England (scoring 30 goals), and was named Football Writers' Association Player of the Year in 1994, and the PFA Player of the Year in 1995. Since retiring as a footballer in 2006 Shearer has worked as a television pundit for the BBC.

Peter David Ebdon
b. 27th August 1970

Professional snooker player who became World Champion in 2002 after beating Stephen Hendry 18-17 in the final. He turned professional in 1991 and impressively reached the quarter-finals of the 1992 World Championship (a run which earned him the WPBSA Young Player of the Year award). Since then, in addition to his 2002 World Championship title, he has won the World Open (1993), Scottish Open (2001), U.K. Championship (2006), and five other ranking events.

Darren Gough
b. 18th September 1970

Retired cricketer and former captain of Yorkshire County Cricket Club. The spearhead of England's bowling attack through much of the 1990s, he is England's second highest wicket-taker in one-day internationals with 234, and took 229 wickets in his 58 Test matches for England. In 2005 he took part in the BBC television series Strictly Come Dancing - partnered with British National champion Lilia Kopylova he went on to win both the main series and the 2005 Christmas Special.

Anne-Marie Duff
b. 8th October 1970

Actress who rose to prominence on television playing Fiona Gallagher on the first two seasons of the black comedy series Shameless (2004-2005) and playing Queen Elizabeth I in the miniseries The Virgin Queen (2006). She earned BAFTA Award nominations for her performances in both Shameless and The Virgin Queen, and also for her roles in the films Nowhere Boy (2009) and Suffragette (2015). Duff is an accomplished theatre actor and has worked extensively with the Royal National Theatre.

Sir Matthew Clive Pinsent, CBE
b. 10th October 1970

Rower and broadcaster who has won an impressive 10 world championship gold medals and four consecutive Olympic gold medals (of which three were with Sir Steve Redgrave) during his career. Pinsent announced his retirement from rowing on the 30th November 2004, and was made a Knight Bachelor in the New Year's Honours list announced on the 31st December 2004. Since retiring from rowing he has worked for the BBC as a sports bulletin presenter and reporter.

Zoe Louise Ball
b. 23rd November 1970

Television and radio personality who began her career as a runner at Granada Television and as a researcher on BSkyB. Since then she has been a presenter on numerous television programs such as Top of the Pops, The Big Breakfast, Live & Kicking, the BRIT Awards, Strictly Come Dancing: It Takes Two, and The One Show. On radio Ball is notable as being the first female to host both the BBC's Radio 1 and Radio 2 Breakfast Shows.

Aled Jones, MBE
b. 29th December 1970

Singer and radio and television presenter. In 1985, as a teenage chorister, he reached widespread fame singing a cover version of "Walking in the Air" for Channel 4's animated film The Snowman. Since then he has become well known for his television work with the BBC and ITV, as well as his radio work (for BBC Radio Wales and Classic FM). In February 2014 Jones was nominated as an Honorary Fellow of the Royal Academy of Music; he was presented with the fellowship on the 3rd July 2014.

NOTEABLE DEATHS

1st Jan	Alfred Lauck Parson (b. 24th October 1889) - Chemist and physicist who in 1915 proposed the magneton theory of the structure of the atom.
4th Jan	David John Williams (b. 26th June 1885) - One of the foremost Welsh-language writers of the twentieth century and a prominent Welsh nationalist.
7th Jan	Allan Wilkie, CBE (b. 9th February 1878) - English Shakespearean actor of Scottish descent who is noted for his career in Australia.
13th Jan	Jimmy Hanley (b. 22nd October 1918) - Film, television and stage actor.
23rd Jan	Sir Ifan ab Owen Edwards (b. 25th July 1895) - Academic, writer and film-maker best known as the founder of Urdd Gobaith Cymru, the Welsh League of Youth.
26th Jan	Sir Albert Cynan Evans-Jones, CBE (b. 14th April 1895) - Poet and dramatist.
29th Jan	Sir Basil Henry Liddell Hart (b. 31st October 1895) - Soldier, military historian and military theorist.
30th Jan	Malcolm Keen (b. 8th August 1887) - Actor of stage, film and television.
2nd Feb	Bertrand Arthur William Russell, 3rd Earl Russell, OM, FRS (b. 18th May 1872) - Philosopher, logician, mathematician, historian, writer, essayist, social critic, political activist and Nobel laureate.
10th Feb	Alfred Roberts, JP (b. 18th April 1892) - Grocer, local preacher and politician whose second daughter Margaret became the first female Prime Minister of the United Kingdom.
14th Feb	Herbert 'Bert' Strudwick (b. 28th January 1880) - English wicket-keeper whose career record of 1493 dismissals is the third-highest by any wicket-keeper in the history of first-class cricket.
15th Feb	Air Chief Marshal Hugh Caswall Tremenheere Dowding, 1st Baron Dowding, GCB, GCVO, CMG (b. 24th April 1882) - Officer in the Royal Air Force and the Air Officer Commanding RAF Fighter Command during the Battle of Britain.
28th Feb	Arthur Henry Knighton-Hammond (b. 18th September 1875) - Painter best known for landscapes, society portraits and industrial paintings.
13th Mar	Alexander Sheriff de Moro 'Alec' Clunes (b. 17th May 1912) - Actor and theatrical manager.
29th Mar	Vera Mary Brittain (b. 29th December 1893) - Voluntary Aid Detachment (VAD) nurse, writer, feminist, socialist and pacifist.
20th Apr	Thomas Iorwerth Ellis, OBE (b. 19th December 1899) - Welsh classicist who was awarded an honorary degree of LLD by the University of Wales in 1967 in recognition of his cultural services to Wales.
21st Apr	General Sir Thomas Lionel Hunton, KCB, OBE, MVO (b. 30th October 1885) - Royal Marines officer who served as the inaugural Commandant General Royal Marines from 1943 until he retired in 1946.
7th May	Jack Jones, CBE (b. 24th November 1884) - Miner, Trade Union official, politician, novelist and playwright.
26th May	Ronald Victor Courtenay Bodley, MC (b. 3rd March 1892) - Army officer, author and journalist who was considered among the most distinguished British writers on the Sahara, as well as one of the main western sources of information on the South Pacific Mandate.

7th Jun	Edward Morgan Forster, OM, CH (b. 1st January 1879) - Novelist, short story writer, essayist and librettist who was nominated for the Nobel Prize in Literature in 16 different years. Some of his most notable novels include Where Angels Fear to Tread (1905), A Room with a View (1908), Howards End (1910) and A Passage to India (1924).
15th Jun	Major-General Sir John Noble Kennedy, GCMG, KCVO, KBE, CB, MC (b. 31st August 1893) - Army officer who served as Assistant Chief of the Imperial General Staff during World War II.
27th Jun	Thomas Edwin La Dell, ARA (b. 7th January 1914) - Printmaker, lithographer, illustrator and painter active during the 1940s, 1950s and 1960s.
30th Jun	Arthur Leslie Scottorn Broughton (b. 8th December 1899) - Actor and playwright best known for playing public house landlord Jack Walker in the television soap opera Coronation Street.
30th Jun	Katherine Githa Sowerby (b. 6th October 1876) - Playwright, children's writer and member of the Fabian Society who is also known under her pen name K. G. Sowerby.
7th Jul	Sir Allen Lane (b. 21st September 1902) - Publisher who together with his brothers Richard and John Lane founded Penguin Books in 1935, bringing high-quality paperback fiction and non-fiction to the mass market.
20th Jul	Iain Norman Macleod (b. 11th November 1913) - Conservative Party politician and government minister.
29th Jul	Sir John Barbirolli, CH (b. 2nd December 1899) - Conductor and cellist who is best remembered as the conductor of the Hallé Orchestra in Manchester.
5th Sep	Jesse Pennington (b. 23rd August 1883) - Football player who played left-back for West Bromwich Albion for 19 years and earned 25 caps for England (including 2 caps as captain).
19th Sep	Greville Thomas Scott Stevens (b. 7th January 1901) - One of the leading amateur cricketers of his generation who played for Middlesex, Oxford University and England.
8th Nov	Alasdair Roderick Mackenzie (b. 3rd August 1903) - Scottish farmer and politician who became a Liberal Member of Parliament.
8th Nov	Huw Thomas Edwards (b. 19th November 1892) - Welsh trade union leader and politician.
13th Nov	Elizabeth Margaret Braddock (b. 24th September 1899) - Labour Party politician won a national reputation for her forthright campaigns in connection with housing, public health and other social issues.
1st Dec	Frank Smailes (b. 27th March 1910) - Cricketer who played first-class cricket for Yorkshire and one Test for England. He was one of Yorkshire's main players in the club's outstanding years when they won eight County Championships out of ten.
8th Dec	Sir Christopher Kelk Ingold, BEM, FRS (b. 28th October 1893) - Chemist who is regarded as one of the chief pioneers of physical organic chemistry.
14th Dec	Field Marshal William Joseph Slim, 1st Viscount Slim, KG, GCB, GCMG, GCVO, GBE, DSO, MC, KStJ (b. 6th August 1891) - British military commander and the 13th Governor-General of Australia.
26th Dec	Lillian Barbara Board, MBE (b. 13th December 1948) - Athlete who won the silver medal in the 400m at the 1968 Summer Olympics in Mexico City.
26th Dec	Henry Colville Montgomery Campbell, KCVO, MC, PC (b. 11th October 1887) - Church of England bishop.
31st Dec	Cyril Meir Scott (b. 27th September 1879) - Composer, writer, poet and occultist.

1970 TOP 10 SINGLES

Mungo Jerry	No.1	In The Summertime
Elvis Presley	No.2	The Wonder Of You
Freda Payne	No.3	Band Of Gold
Norman Greenbaum	No.4	Spirit In The Sky
Simon & Garfunkel	No.5	Bridge Over Troubled Water
England World Cup Squad	No.6	Back Home
Free	No.7	All Right Now
Lee Marvin	No.8	Wand'rin' Star
Christie	No.9	Yellow River
Smokey Robinson & The Miracles	No.10	The Tears Of A Clown

① Mungo Jerry
In The Summertime

Label:	Written by:	Length:
Dawn Records	Ray Dorset	3 mins 40 secs

Mungo Jerry are a British rock group who experienced their greatest success in the early 1970s. With a changing line-up that has always been fronted by Ray Dorset, they have had nine charting singles in the U.K., including two No.1's. The group's biggest hit was 'In The Summertime' which became one of the best-selling singles of all-time, eventually selling in excess of 30 million copies.

---

② Elvis Presley
The Wonder Of You

Label:	Written by:	Length:
RCA Victor	Baker Knight	2 mins 37 secs

Elvis Aaron Presley (b. 8th January 1935 - d. 16th August 1977) was an American singer and actor. Regarded as one of the most significant cultural icons and influential musicians of the 20th century, he is often referred to as the King of Rock and Roll, or simply, the King. 'The Wonder of You' was one of Elvis's most successful records in the U.K. ever, topping the Singles Chart for six weeks in the summer of 1970.

③ Freda Payne
Band Of Gold

Label:	Written by:	Length:
Invictus	Wayne / Dunbar	2 mins 50 secs

Freda Charcilia Payne (b. 19th September 1942) is an American singer and actress in musicals and film who is best known for her career in music from the mid-1960s through to the mid-1980s. Her most notable record is her 1970 pop smash 'Band Of Gold' which reached No.1 on the Singles Chart for six consecutive weeks in September 1970. Payne is the older sister of Scherrie Payne, a former singer with the American vocal group The Supremes.

---

④ Norman Greenbaum
Spirit In The Sky

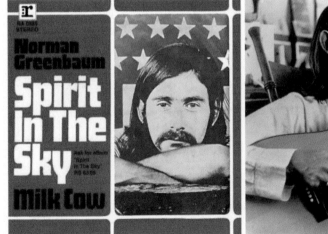 

Label:	Written by:	Length:
Reprise Records	Norman Greenbaum	3 mins 57 secs

Norman Joel Greenbaum (b. 20th November 1942) is an American singer-songwriter who is best known for writing and performing the 1969 song 'Spirit in the Sky'. The song, which sold two million copies in 1969 and 1970, has subsequently been used in many films, advertisements and television shows.

Simon & Garfunkel
Bridge Over Troubled Water

Label:	Written by:	Length:
CBS	Paul Simon	4 mins 57 secs

Simon & Garfunkel were a folk-rock duo consisting of singer-songwriter Paul Simon and singer Art Garfunkel. They were one of the best-selling music groups of the 1960s and became counterculture icons of the decade's social revolution alongside artists such as the Beatles, the Beach Boys and Bob Dylan. Their biggest hits - including The Sound Of Silence (1964), Mrs. Robinson (1968), The Boxer (1969) and Bridge Over Troubled Water (1970) - reached No.1 on singles charts worldwide. Simon & Garfunkel won 10 Grammy Awards in total and were inducted into the Rock and Roll Hall of Fame in 1990.

England World Cup Squad
Back Home

Label:	Written by:	Length:
Pye Records	Martin / Coulter	2 mins 7 secs

Back Home was recorded by the 1970 England World Cup squad and reached No.1 in the U.K. Singles Chart for three weeks in May 1970. Written and produced by Bill Martin and Phil Coulter, the single began the tradition of the England squad recording World Cup songs to celebrate their involvement in the competition. The B side of the 7" single was called 'Cinnamon Stick' and was also sung by the England football team.

7

Free
All Right Now

Label:	Written by:	Length:
Island Records	Fraser / Rodgers	4 mins 13 secs

Free were an English rock band consisting of Paul Rodgers (lead vocals), Paul Kossoff (lead guitarist) Andy Fraser (bass guitar) and Simon Kirke (drums). Formed in London in 1968, Free are best known for their 1970 signature song 'All Right Now'. The group disbanded in 1973, by which time they had sold more than 20 million albums around the world and played more than 700 arena and festival concerts.

8

Lee Marvin
Wand'rin' Star

Label:	Written by:	Length:
Paramount Records	Lerner / Loewe	2 mins 58 secs

Lee Marvin (b. 19th February 1924 - d. 29th August 1987) was an American film and television actor who had a one-hit wonder in March 1970 with 'Wand'rin' Star'. The song was originally written by Alan J. Lerner (lyrics) and Frederick Loewe (music) for the stage musical Paint Your Wagon in 1951. When the film of the musical was made in 1969 Marvin took the role of prospector Ben Rumson and, although not a natural singer, sang all of his songs in the film. Despite the film being a box office flop the soundtrack was a success and Wand'rin' Star became a No.1 hit in both the U.K. and Ireland.

⑨ Christie
Yellow River

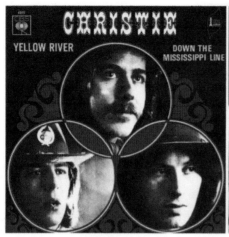

Label:	Written by:	Length:
CBS	Jeff Christie	2 mins 43 secs

Christie is an English rock band that formed at the end of the 1960s. In June 1970 band members Jeff Christie (vocals, bass), Vic Elmes (guitar) and Michael Blakley (drums) made it to the top the U.K. Singles Chart with their record 'Yellow River'. Written by band leader Jeff Christie, the song was a worldwide smash and made it to No.1 in 26 countries.

---

⑩ Smokey Robinson & The Miracles
The Tears Of A Clown

Label:	Written by:	Length:
Tamla Motown	Cosby / Wonder / Robinson	2 mins 56 secs

Smokey Robinson & The Miracles were an American rhythm and blues vocal group that was the first successful recording act for Berry Gordy's Motown Records. They were one of the most important and influential groups in pop, rock and roll, and R&B music history, and were inducted to the Vocal Group Hall of Fame in 2001. 'The Tears of a Clown', written by Hank Cosby, Smokey Robinson and Stevie Wonder, became an international multi-million seller and was inducted into the Grammy Hall of Fame in 2002.

1970: TOP FILMS

1. **Love Story** - *Paramount*
2. **Airport** - *Universal*
3. **M*A*S*H** - *20th Century Fox*
4. **Patton** - *20th Century Fox*
5. **Little Big Man** - *Warner Bros.*

OSCARS

Best Picture: Patton

Most Nominations: Patton (10) / Airport (10)

Most Wins: Patton (7)

Glenda Jackson / Frank McCarthy appearing for Best Actor George C. Scott.

Best Director: Franklin J. Schaffner - *Patton*

Best Actor: George C. Scott (award declined) - *Patton*
Best Actress: Glenda Jackson - *Women In Love*
Best Supporting Actor: John Mills - *Ryan's Daughter*
Best Supporting Actress: Helen Hayes - *Airport*

The 43rd Academy Awards, honouring the best in film for 1970, were presented on the 15th April 1971 at the Dorothy Chandler Pavilion in Los Angeles, California.

LOVE STORY

love means never having to say you're sorry—

PARAMOUNT PICTURES PRESENTS

Ali MacGraw • Ryan O'Neal

The Year's
#1
Best Seller

A HOWARD G. MINSKY - ARTHUR HILLER Production

Directed by: Arthur Hiller - Runtime: 1 hour 40 minutes

Harvard Law student Oliver Barrett IV and music student Jennifer Cavilleri fall in love despite their different backgrounds and upbringing, and then tragedy strikes.

STARRING

Ali MacGraw
b. 1st April 1939

Character:
Jennifer Cavilleri

Ryan O'Neal
b. 20th April 1941

Character:
Oliver Barrett IV

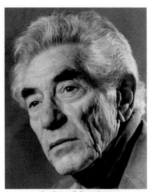

John Marley
b. 17th October 1907
d. 22nd May 1984

Character:
Phil Cavaleri

TRIVIA

Interesting Facts

Author Erich Segal wrote the screenplay first and then adapted it into a novel. It was published before the film's release and became a runaway bestseller.

The scenes with Oliver walking alone through a snowy New York were added after principal photography had been completed. The production was almost out of money and did not have the necessary funds for permits to shoot in New York City again - so all the shots were grabbed 'illegally' using a skeleton film crew and Ryan O'Neal.

To prepare for their roles Ryan O'Neal learned to ice skate and Ali MacGraw learned to play the harpsichord.

This movie marked the first film appearance of Ray Milland (Oliver Barrett III) without the hairpiece that he had worn for decades.

Eight up-and-coming actors including Michael Douglas, Jon Voight and Peter Fonda turned down the role of Oliver despite being offered 10% of the gross.

The film features the only Oscar nominated performances of Ali MacGraw, Ryan O'Neal and John Marley.

Quotes

[first lines]
Oliver Barrett IV: What can you say about a twenty-five-year-old girl who died? That she was beautiful and brilliant? That she loved Mozart and Bach, the Beatles, and me?

Oliver Barrett IV: Jenny... I'm sorry.
Jennifer Cavalieri: Don't. Love means never having to say you're sorry.

AIRPORT

Directed by: George Seaton - Runtime: 2 hours 17 minutes

Mel Bakersfeld, the general manager of a midwestern airport, must contend with a massive snowstorm and other issues while the troubled D.O. Guerrero threatens to blow up an airliner.

STARRING

Burt" Lancaster
b. 2ⁿᵈ November 1913
d. 20ᵗʰ October 1994
Character:
Mel Bakersfeld

Dean Martin
b. 7ᵗʰ June 1917
d. 25ᵗʰ December 1995
Character:
Vernon Demerest

Jean Seberg
b. 13ᵗʰ November 1938
d. 30ᵗʰ August 1979
Character:
Tanya Livingston

TRIVIA

Interesting Facts

The cast includes five Oscar winners: Burt Lancaster, Van Heflin, George Kennedy, Helen Hayes and Maureen Stapleton.

Burt Lancaster made a great deal of money from Airport being a huge hit. His contract gave him a 10% profit participation once the film made over $50 million; it grossed in excess of $100 million. Despite the financial windfall Lancaster said that the movie was "the worst piece of junk ever made." He said he only made this film in return for the studio agreeing to finance several non-commercial films in which he was interested.

In shots of the airport terminal, ticket counters for Northwest Orient Airlines, Western Airlines, Pan Am, TWA, and Continental Airlines can be seen. None of those airlines are in operation today due to bankruptcy or mergers.

The passenger sitting right behind Ada Quonsett (played by Helen Hayes) is Pat Priest (as the uncredited Mrs. J. Copeland). Priest is best known for portraying Marilyn Munster on the television show The Munsters (1964-1966).

When Helen Hayes won the Best Supporting Actress Oscar for this film two of the other nominees were Karen Black and Lee Grant. Black went on to appear in Airport 1975 (1974) and Grant in Airport '77 (1977).

Quotes

Capt. Vernon Demerest: According to the manifest there's three doctors on board.
Captain Anson Harris: Let's hope they're not dentists.

Ada Quonsett: My late husband played the violin. Not professionally, but he was very good. He once played the Minute Waltz in 58 seconds.

M*A*S*H

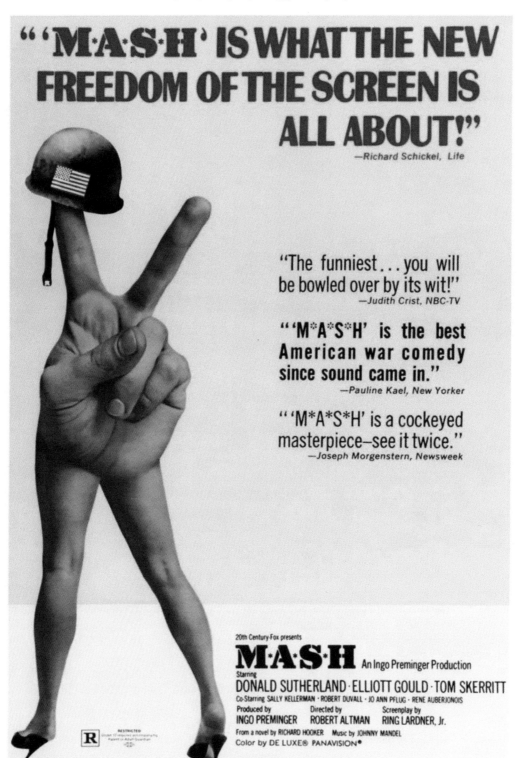

"'M·A·S·H' IS WHAT THE NEW FREEDOM OF THE SCREEN IS ALL ABOUT!"
—Richard Schickel, Life

"The funniest...you will be bowled over by its wit!"
—Judith Crist, NBC-TV

"'M*A*S*H' is the best American war comedy since sound came in."
—Pauline Kael, New Yorker

"'M*A*S*H' is a cockeyed masterpiece—see it twice."
—Joseph Morgenstern, Newsweek

20th Century-Fox presents

M·A·S·H An Ingo Preminger Production

Starring
DONALD SUTHERLAND · ELLIOTT GOULD · TOM SKERRITT

Co-Starring SALLY KELLERMAN · ROBERT DUVALL · JO ANN PFLUG · RENE AUBERJONOIS

Produced by INGO PREMINGER   Directed by ROBERT ALTMAN   Screenplay by RING LARDNER, Jr.

From a novel by RICHARD HOOKER   Music by JOHNNY MANDEL

Color by DE LUXE® PANAVISION®

R RESTRICTED

Directed by: Robert Altman - Runtime: 1 hour 56 minutes

The staff of a Korean War field hospital use humour and high jinks to keep their sanity in the face of the horror of war.

STARRING

Donald Sutherland
b. 17th July 1935

Character:
Hawkeye Pierce

Elliott Gould
b. 29th August 1938

Character:
Trapper John McIntyre

Tom Skerritt
b. 25th August 1933

Character:
Duke Forrest

TRIVIA

Goofs When Hot Lips O'Houlihan (Sally Kellerman) confronts Lt. Col. Blake (Roger Bowen) after she was exposed in the shower, she stands framed in the doorway of Lt. Col. Blake's tent. To her left there is a mirror hanging on the tent wall which appears and disappears between shots.

Interesting Facts The fourteen-year-old son of director Robert Altman, Mike, wrote the lyrics to the theme song 'Suicide is Painless'. Because of its inclusion in the subsequent television series he continued to get royalties throughout its run and syndication. His father was paid $75,000 for directing the film but his son eventually made around $2 million in royalties from the song.

In the opening titles you see a soldier carrying a wounded soldier on a stretcher. The soldier then accidentally trips and falls down, this wasn't scripted. Robert Altman decided that instead of editing it out of the scene he would use it to foreshadow the movies dark humour theme.

Screenwriter Ring Lardner Jr. was very upset when he saw how very little of his original script made it into the final cut. He allegedly told Elliott Gould, "There's not a word that I wrote on screen". Lardner later won an Academy Award for his screenplay (the films' only Oscar from five nominations).

Quotes *[a gun goes off at the football game]*
Hotlips O'Houlihan: Oh my God! They've shot him!
Colonel Blake: Hot Lips, you incredible nincompoop! It's the end of the quarter.

Duke Forrest: *[as Frank Burns is being taken away in a straightjacket]* Now, fair's fair Henry. If I nail Hotlips and hit Hawkeye can I go home too?

Patton

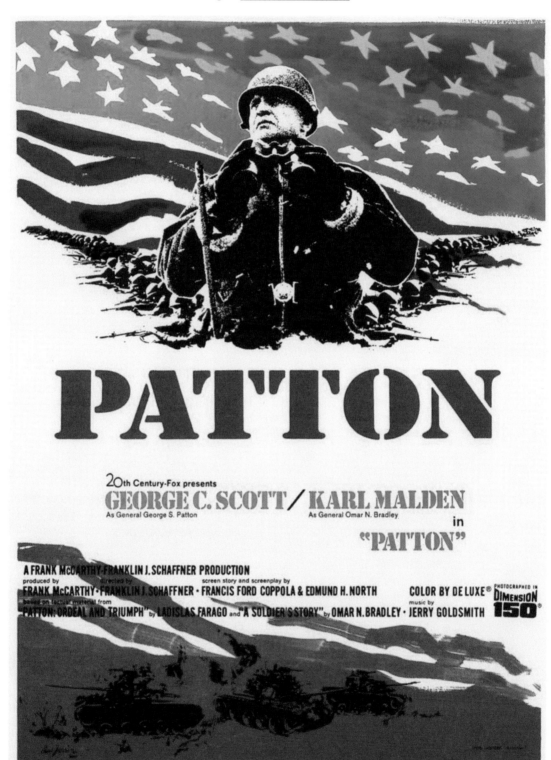

Directed by: Franklin J. Schaffner - Runtime: 2 hours 52 minutes

The World War II phase of the career of the controversial American general George S. Patton.

STARRING

George C. Scott
b. 18th October 1927
d. 22nd September 1999
Character:
General George S. Patton

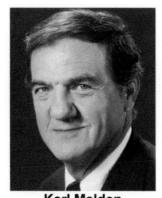

Karl Malden
b.22nd March 1912
d. 1st July 2009
Character:
General Omar N. Bradley

Stephen Young
b. 19th May 1939

Character:
Captain Chester Hansen

TRIVIA

Goofs | Although the film is set during World War II, the map of Europe seen in the headquarters is post war and shows an already divided Germany.

Interesting Facts | The ivory-handled revolvers George C. Scott wears in the opening speech were actually George S. Patton's bona-fide revolvers.

Producer Frank McCarthy was a retired brigadier general who served on the staff of General George C. Marshall during World War II, and worked for 20 years to make a film about George S. Patton. After winning the Academy Award for Best Picture in 1971, McCarthy donated his Oscar to the George C. Marshall Museum at the Virginia Military Institute.

About 16 and a half minutes into the film Patton's jeep rides through the desert with a placard displaying the letters 'WTF'. This stands for Western Task Force, rather than the more modern acronym that uses those same letters.

George C. Scott won the Academy Award for best actor and famously refused to accept it. He claimed that competition between actors was unfair and a "meat parade".

Quotes | *[first lines]*
Patton: Now I want you to remember that no bastard ever won a war by dying for his country. He won it by making the other poor dumb bastard die for his country.

Clergyman: I was interested to see a Bible by your bed. You actually find time to read it?
Patton: I sure do. Every goddamn day.

LITTLE BIG MAN

Directed by: Arthur Penn - Runtime: 2 hours 19 minutes

121-year-old Jack Crabb recounts his life being raised by Native Americans through to him becoming a scout for General George Custer at the Battle of the Little Bighorn.

STARRING

Dustin Hoffman
b. 8th August 1937

Character:
Jack Crabb

Faye Dunaway
b. 14th January 1941

Character:
Mrs. Pendrake

Chief Dan George
b. 24th July 1899
d. 23rd September 1981

Character:
Old Lodge Skins

TRIVIA

Revealing Mistakes

The wires forcing a horse to fall are visible in the final battle scene, just before Custer exclaims "Fools! They're shooting their own horses!".

Interesting Facts

In order to get the raspy voice of 121-year-old Jack, Dustin Hoffman sat in his dressing room and screamed at the top of his lungs for an hour.

Little Big Man was the name of an actual historical figure. He was a Native American, an Oglala Lakota, who was a fearless and respected warrior. He fought under, and was rivals with, Crazy Horse. He also fought at the Battle of Little Big Horn.

Old Lodge Skins' (Chief Dan George's) line "Today, is a good day to die", was adopted by the Star Trek Universe as a Klingon's catchphrase.

Chief Dan George became the first Native American to receive an Academy Award nomination for acting.

Quotes

Jack Crabb: Grandfather, I have a white wife.
Old Lodge Skins: You do? That's interesting. Does she cook and does she work hard?
Jack Crabb: Yes, Grandfather.
Old Lodge Skins: That surprises me. Does she show pleasant enthusiasm when you mount her?
Jack Crabb: Well sure, Grandfather.
Old Lodge Skins: That surprises me even more. I tried one of them once but she didn't show any enthusiasm at all.

Old Lodge Skins: Today is a good day to die.

SPORTING WINNERS

B B C SPORTS PERSONALITY OF THE YEAR

HENRY COOPER - BOXING

Sir Henry Cooper, OBE, KSG (b. 3rd May 1934 - d. 1st May 2011) was a heavyweight boxer who held the British, Commonwealth, and European heavyweight titles several times throughout his career, and unsuccessfully challenged Muhammad Ali for the world heavyweight championship in 1966. He is the only British boxer to win three Lonsdale Belts outright.

Professional Boxing Record:

		Knockout	Decision	Disqualification
Wins	40	27	11	2
Losses	14	8	5	1
Draws	1	-	-	-

Cooper was the first person to win the BBC Sports Personality of the Year award twice (in 1967 and 1970) and is today one of only four two-time winners in the award's history; he won the 1970 award after becoming the British, Commonwealth, and European heavyweight champion.

1970	BBC Sports Personality Results	Country	Sport
Winner	**Henry Cooper**	**England**	**Boxing**
Runner Up	Tony Jacklin	England	Golf
Third Place	Bobby Moore	England	Football

Following his retirement from boxing Cooper continued his career as a television and radio personality. He also appeared in various television adverts, most famously in those for Brut aftershave.

FIVE NATIONS RUGBY WINNERS

FRANCE & WALES

Position	Nation	Played	Won	Draw	Lost	For	Against	+/-	Points
1	**France**	**4**	**3**	**0**	**1**	**60**	**33**	**+27**	**6**
1	**Wales**	**4**	**3**	**0**	**1**	**46**	**42**	**+4**	**6**
3	Ireland	4	2	0	2	33	28	+5	4
4	Scotland	4	1	0	3	43	50	-7	2
5	England	4	1	0	3	40	69	-19	2

The 1970 Five Nations Championship was the forty-first series of the rugby union Five Nations Championship. Including the previous incarnations as the Home Nations and Five Nations, this was the seventy-sixth series of the northern hemisphere rugby union championship.

Date	Team		Score		Team	Location
10-01-1970	Scotland		9-11		France	Edinburgh
24-01-1970	France		8-0		Ireland	Paris
07-02-1970	Wales		18-9		Scotland	Cardiff
14-02-1970	England		9-3		Ireland	London
28-02-1970	England		13-17		Wales	London
28-02-1970	Ireland		16-11		Scotland	Dublin
14-03-1970	Ireland		14-0		Wales	Dublin
21-03-1970	Scotland		14-5		England	Edinburgh
04-04-1970	Wales		11-6		France	Cardiff
18-04-1970	France		35-13		England	Paris

CALCUTTA CUP

SCOTLAND 14 - 5 ENGLAND

The Calcutta Cup was first awarded in 1879 and is the rugby union trophy awarded to the winner of the match (currently played as part of the Six Nations Championship) between England and Scotland. The Cup was presented to the Rugby Football Union after the Calcutta Football Club in India disbanded in 1878; it is made from melted down silver rupees withdrawn from the club's funds.

BRITISH GRAND PRIX - JOCHEN RINDT

Jochen Rindt being presented with his trophy after winning the British Grand Prix.

The 1970 British Grand Prix was held at Brands Hatch on the 18th July. The race was won by German born Austrian driver Jochen Rindt, from pole position, over 80 laps of the 2.65-mile circuit. Australian Jack Brabham took the fastest lap with a time of 1m 25.9s.

Pos.	Country	Driver	Car
1	**Austria**	**Jochen Rindt**	**Lotus-Ford**
2	Australia	Jack Brabham	Brabham-Ford
3	New Zealand	Denny Hulme	McLaren-Ford

1970 GRAND PRIX SEASON

Date	Grand Prix	Circuit	Winning Driver	Constructor
07-03	South African	Kyalami	Jack Brabham	Brabham-Ford
19-04	Spanish	Jarama	Jackie Stewart	March-Ford
10-05	Monaco	Monaco	Jochen Rindt	Lotus-Ford
07-06	Belgian	Spa-Francorchamps	Pedro Rodríguez	BRM
21-06	Dutch	Zandvoort	Jochen Rindt	Lotus-Ford
05-07	French	Charade	Jochen Rindt	Lotus-Ford
18-07	British	Brands Hatch	Jochen Rindt	Lotus-Ford
02-08	German	Hockenheimring	Jochen Rindt	Lotus-Ford
16-08	Austrian	Österreichring	Jacky Ickx	Ferrari
06-09	Italian	Monza	Clay Regazzoni	Ferrari
20-09	Canadian	Mont-Tremblant	Jacky Ickx	Ferrari
04-10	United States	Watkins Glen	Emerson Fittipaldi	Lotus-Ford
25-10	Mexican	Magdalena Mixhuca	Jacky Ickx	Ferrari

The 1970 Formula One season was the 24th season of the FIA's Formula One motor racing. It featured the 21st World Championship of Drivers which was won by Jochen Rindt (awarded posthumously) with 45 points, from Jacky Ickx (40) and Clay Regazzoni (33). It also featured the 13th International Cup for F1 Manufacturers which was won by Lotus.

GRAND NATIONAL - GAY TRIP

The 1970 Grand National was the 124th renewal of this world famous horse race and took place at Aintree Racecourse near Liverpool on the 4th April. Gay Trip won the race by 20 lengths and was ridden by jockey Pat Taaffe.

Of the 28 horses that contested the race only 7 completed it; 11 fell, 4 were brought down, 3 refused and 3 unseated their riders.

Photo: Victorious Irish jockey Pat Taaffe rides Gay Trip through cheering crowds after winning the 1970 Grand National.

	Horse	Jockey	Age	Weight	Odds
1st	**Gay Trip**	**Pat Taaffe**	**8**	**11st-5lb**	**15/1**
2nd	Vulture	Sean Barker	8	10st-0lb	15/1
3rd	Miss Hunter	Frank Shortt	9	10st-0lb	33/1
4th	Dozo	Eddie Harty	9	10st-4lb	100/8
5th	Ginger Nut	Jimmy Bourke	8	10st-0lb	28/1

EPSOM DERBY - NIJINSKY

The Derby Stakes is Britain's richest horse race and the most prestigious of the country's five Classics. First run in 1780 this Group 1 flat horse race is open to 3-year-old thoroughbred colts and fillies. The race takes place at Epsom Downs in Surrey over a distance of one mile, four furlongs and 10 yards (2,423 metres) and is scheduled for early June each year.

Photo: Canadian-bred, Irish-trained Thoroughbred racehorse and sire Nijinsky (1967-1992) seen being led in after winning the 1970 Epsom Derby. The horse was owned by Charles W. Engelhard, Jr., trained by Vincent O'Brien and ridden by Lester Piggott.

FOOTBALL LEAGUE CHAMPIONS

England

Pos.	Team	W	D	L	F	A	Pts.
1	**Everton**	**29**	**8**	**5**	**72**	**34**	**66**
2	Leeds United	21	15	6	84	49	57
3	Chelsea	21	13	8	70	50	55
4	Derby County	22	9	11	64	37	53
5	Liverpool	20	11	11	65	42	51

Scotland

Pos.	Team	W	D	L	F	A	Pts.
1	**Celtic**	**27**	**3**	**4**	**96**	**33**	**57**
2	Rangers	19	7	8	67	40	45
3	Hibernian	19	6	9	65	40	44
4	Heart of Midlothian	13	12	9	50	36	38
5	Dundee United	16	6	12	62	64	38

FA CUP WINNERS - CHELSEA

Date	Played At	Team	Score	Team	Attendance
11th April	Wembley Stadium	Chelsea	2-2	Leeds United	100,000
29th April	Old Trafford	Chelsea	2-1	Leeds United	62,078

County Championship Cricket Winners

The 1970 County Championship was the 71st officially organised running of this cricket competition and saw Kent win their fifth title.

Pos.	Team	Played	Won	Lost	Drawn	Batting Bonus	Bowling Bonus	Points
1	**Kent**	**24**	**9**	**5**	**10**	**70**	**77**	**237**
2	Glamorgan	24	9	6	9	48	82	220
3	Lancashire	24	6	2	16	78	78	216
4	Yorkshire	24	8	5	11	49	86	215
5	Surrey	24	6	4	14	60	83	203

First Class Cricket

England   1-4   Rest of the World

Game	Ground	Result
1	Lord's, London	Rest of the World won by an innings and 80 runs
2	Trent Bridge, Nottingham	England won by 8 wickets
3	Edgbaston, Birmingham	Rest of the World won by 5 wickets
4	Headingley, Leeds	Rest of the World won by 2 wickets
5	The Oval, London	Rest of the World won by 4 wickets

Golf - Open Championship - Jack Nicklaus

The 1970 Open Championship was the 99th to be played and was held between the 8th and 12th July at the Old Course in St Andrews, Scotland. Jack Nicklaus prevailed in an 18-hole Sunday playoff over fellow American Doug Sanders, winning the second of his three Opens and £5,250 in prize money.

Photo: Jack Nicklaus (and his wife Barbara) with the Claret Jug after winning the 1970 British Open Golf Championship.

WIMBLEDON

Photo 1: John Newcombe kisses his men's singles trophy. Photo 2: Margaret Court holds the victor's trophy plate after winning the women's singles final.

Men's Singles Champion: John Newcombe - Australia
Ladies Singles Champion: Margaret Court - Australia

The 1970 Wimbledon Championships was the 84th staging of tournament and took place on the outdoor grass courts at the All England Lawn Tennis and Croquet Club in Wimbledon, London. It ran from the 22nd June until the 4th July and was the third Grand Slam tennis event of 1970.

Men's Singles Final:

Country	Player	Set 1	Set 2	Set 3	Set 4	Set 5
Australia	John Newcombe	5	6	6	3	6
Australia	Ken Rosewall	7	3	2	6	1

Women's Singles Final:

Country	Player	Set 1	Set 2
Australia	Margaret Court	14	11
United States	Billie Jean King	12	9

Men's Doubles Final:

Country	Players	Set 1	Set 2	Set 3
Australia	John Newcombe / Tony Roche	10	6	6
Australia	Ken Rosewall / Fred Stolle	8	3	1

Women's Doubles Final:

Country	Players	Set 1	Set 2
United States	Rosie Casals / Billie Jean King	6	6
France / United Kingdom	Françoise Dürr / Virginia Wade	2	3

Mixed Doubles Final:

Country	Players	Set 1	Set 2	Set 3
Romania / United States	Ilie Năstase / Rosie Casals	6	4	9
Soviet Union	Alex Metreveli / Olga Morozova	3	6	7

SNOOKER - RAY REARDON

Ray Reardon 37 - 33 John Pulman

The 1970 World Snooker Championship was held at the Victoria Hall in London from the 6th-11th April. Ray Reardon won in the final against John Pulman to take the first of his six world titles (1970, 1973, 1974, 1975, 1976 and 1978) and £1,225 in prize money. He also made the highest break of the tournament with 118. *Photo: John Pulman (left) and Ray Reardon during the 1970 Snooker World Championship final.*

1970 COMMONWEALTH GAMES

The 1970 British Commonwealth Games were held in Edinburgh from the 16th-25th July. It was the first-time metric units rather than imperial units were used in all events, and also the first time the games were held in Scotland.

Medals Table:

Rank	Nation	Gold	Silver	Bronze	Total
1	**Australia**	**36**	**24**	**22**	**82**
2	England	27	25	32	84
3	Canada	18	24	24	66
4	Scotland	6	8	11	25
5	Kenya	5	3	6	14
10	Northern Ireland	3	1	5	9
12	Wales	2	6	4	12

THE COST OF LIVING

PLAYER'S Nº10

Enjoy all the satisfaction of specially selected
Virginia tobaccos in a cigarette of guaranteed quality.
Enjoy easier saving too – because Player's Nº10 coupons can be
used with coupons from Player's Nº6.

Guaranteed
quality
plus coupons
3'6
RECOMMENDED PRICE

COMPARISON CHART

	1970	1970 (+ Inflation)	2019	% Change
3 Bedroom House	£5,800	£93,896	£236,676	+152.1%
Weekly Income	£13.3s.1d	£212.95	£569	+167.2%
Pint Of Beer	1s.4d	£1.08	£3.69	+241.7%
Cheese (lb)	6s.6d	£5.26	£3.09	-41.2%
Bacon (lb)	7s.9d	£6.27	£2.65	-57.7%
The Beano	4d	27p	£2.75	+918.5%

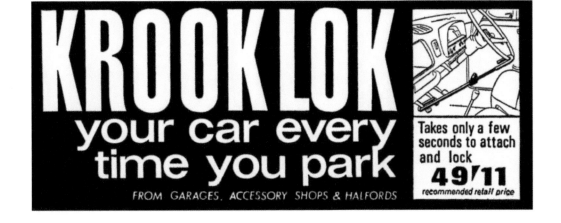

SHOPPING

Danish Lurpak Butter (½lb)	1s.9d
Tesco Creamery Butter (½lb)	1s.5d
Stork Margarine (½lb)	10d
Australian Cheddar Cheese (per lb)	2s.8d
Epicure Pickled Onions (30oz)	4s.2d
Evaporated Milk	1s
Scott's Porage Oats (1½lb)	1s.6d
Golden Delicious Apples (2lbs)	2s.10d
Jaffa Oranges (6)	2s.11d
Spanish Grapes (per lb)	1s.10d
Beef - Topside / Silverside (per lb)	7s.6d
Oven Ready Chicken (per lb)	2s.6d
Danish Bacon - Streaky Rashers (per lb)	3s.8d
Fine Fare Steak & Kidney Pie (15½oz)	2s.9d
Fray Bentos Braised Steak (15oz tin)	3s.8d
Batchelors Peas (19oz)	1s
Tesco Tinned Tomatoes (14½oz)	11d
Heinz Baked Beans (16oz)	1s
Crosse & Blackwell Baked Beans (16oz)	11d
Findus Frozen Sprouts (12oz)	2s.9d
Frozen Sliced Green Beans (16oz)	2s.8d
Sainsbury's Instant Mash Potato	1s
Heinz Tomato Soup (medium tin)	1s.1d
Oxo Cubes (12)	2s.1d
Tom Piper Canned Dessert Puddings	1s.6d
Libby's Creamed Rice (15½oz)	11d
Key Markets Pears In Syrup (29oz)	2s.9d
Peach Slices (15oz)	1s.7d
Ski Low Fat Yogurt	9d
Chivers Jelly	10d
PG Tips (2x ¼lb)	2s.9d
Typhoo Tea (¼lb)	1s.4d
Nescafe Instant Coffee (4oz)	4s.4d
Sunfresh Orange Drink	2s.3d
Tesco Blackcurrant Drink (12floz)	2s.6d
Sainburys Cola (11½floz)	10d
McVitie's Jaffa Cakes	1s.8d
KitKats (6 pack)	1s.8d
Shortcake Biscuits (8oz)	8d
Sainsburys Strawberry Jam (1lb)	1s.7d
Maclean's Toothpaste	3s.3d
Rimmel Beauty Hand Cream	3s.3d
Andrex Toilet Roll (twin pack)	1s.7d
Ariel Washing Powder (giant size)	3s.4d
Ajax (large)	1s.1d
Shift Oven Cleaner (8½oz)	2s.11d
Faithful Dog Food (large tin)	1s.10d

CLOTHES

Women's Clothing

Tweed Raincoat - Quilted Lining	£6.9s.6d
Luxurious Lurex Dress	£4.19s.6d
Courtelle Cardigan	£2.19s
R. J. Wiltshire Crimplene ¾ Lined Skirt	£1.7s.6d
Crimplene Wash 'n' Wear Slacks	£2.15s

Men's Clothing

READY-TO-WEAR SUITS

SAVE £5
~~£16.19.0~~
£11.19.0

SAVE £5
~~£18.19.0~~
£13.19.0

SELECTION FROM OUR WORSTED/'TERYLENE' RANGES

MADE-TO-MEASURE SUITS

SAVE £3
~~£19.19.0~~
£16.19.0

SAVE £5
~~£24.0.0~~
£19.0.0

SAVE £4
~~£22.0.0~~
£18.0.0

SPECIALLY SELECTED CLOTHS INCLUDING FINE WORSTEDS & 'TERYLENE'/WORSTED

SPORTS TROUSERS
USUAL PRICE 75/- NOW **39/6**
ALMOST HALF PRICE!
OTHERS REDUCED TO 49'6 - 59'6

SUPER GRADE WORSTED
MADE-TO-MEASURE SUITS
~~£29.15.0~~
£23.15.0 SAVE £6

SELECTION OF
CAR COATS AND **OVERCOATS** FROM
£8.14.6

LARGE VARIETY OF RAINCOATS FROM
£8.19.0

SPORTS JACKETS
~~£7.19.0~~ to ~~£9.19.0~~
FROM
99/6

DINNER SUITS
~~£19.19.0~~
NOW ONLY
£16.19.0

TOYS

TT Moto-Cross Tri-ang Cycle	£16.19s.6d
Smiley Pedal Car	£5.5s
Woolworths Dolls Pram	£4.19s.6d
Modern Miss Doll	£2.9s.6d
Fuzzy Squirrel Soft Toy	£1.9s.6d
Jolly Jacko Monkey	£2.9s.11d
Telephone Intercom Set	£3.17s.6d
Winfield Table Tennis Set	15s
Matchbox Superfast Loop Set	18s.6d
Jaguar Saloon High Power Friction Car	13s.6d
Super Bubble Kit	5s

ELECTRICAL ITEMS

PYE 24in Television	£77
20in GEC Television	59½gns
Westminster Radiogram	29½gns
Philips Battery Cassette Tape Recorder	22gns
Bush Radio	£8.19s.6d
Electrolux Fridge Freezer (3.4cu.ft.)	29½gns
Servis Supertwin Washer-Spin Dryer	71gns
Electrolux Upright 160 Vacuum Cleaner	£34.3s
Russell Hobbs Kettle	£6.19s.6d
Philips One Pint Coffee Maker	£7.12s.6d
Sunbeam Two Slice Toaster	£7.19s.6d
Electric Can Opener	£6.10s
Philips Hand Hair Dryer	£5.15s
Hair Clippers	£3.17s.6d
Washable Electric Blanket	£11.11s
Philishave Electric Shaver	£6.15s
Ladyshave De Luxe	£4.19s.6d
Black & Decker Electric Drill	£4.15s

OTHER PRICES

Rolls-Royce Silver Shadow Car	£9,272
Vauxhall Viva Deluxe 2-Door Car	£851
3 Day Weekend Tour - Paris	£12.10s
1 Week Prestatyn Holiday Camp (full board)	from £11
10 Day Holiday - St. Aygulf French Riviera	£38
15 Day Holiday - Tossa De Mar, Costa Brava	30gns
Vistorama Grand Tourer Family Tent	36gns
Silver Mist Imperial 7ft x 5ft Shed	£21
Qualcast Superlite Panther Roller Mower	£8.19s.6d
Chester 3 Piece Suite	59½gns
Humber Dining Set	49½gns
Slumberland 4ft 6in Divan Bed	£39.19s.6d
Kumfybunk Bunk Beds	22½gns
Blyth Bedroom Suite	49½gns
Dawmet Elegant Commode Stool	£2.19s.6d
Zenith SLR Camera	£18.19s.6d
Kodak Instamatic Camera	£4.19s.5d
Prinz 12x50 Binoculars	£8.15s
Men's Automatic Timex Watch	£7.15s
Women's High Fashion Timex Watch	£4.10s
White Horse Scotch Whisky	£2.9s.11d
Gordons Gin	£2.9s.11d
Seagers Cream Australian Sherry	13s.9d
Pomagne Champagne Cider	7s.6d
Benson & Hedges Gold Bond Cigarettes (20)	4s.6d
Rothmans Cambridge Cigarettes (20)	4s.6d
Piccadilly No.7 Cigarettes (20)	3s.11d
Woman's Weekly Magazine	9d

New Triumph Toledo: A quality car for £889.

MONEY CONVERSION TABLE

Pounds / Shillings / Pence 'Old Money'		Decimal Value	Value 2019 (Rounded)
Farthing	¼d	0.1p	2p
Half Penny	½d	0.21p	3p
Penny	1d	0.42p	7p
Threepence	3d	1.25p	20p
Sixpence	6d	2.5p	40p
Shilling	1s	5p	81p
Florin	2s	10p	£1.62
Half Crown	2s.6d	12.5p	£2.02
Crown	5s	25p	£4.05
Ten Shillings	10s	50p	£8.09
Pound	20s	£1	£16.19
Guinea	21s	£1.05	£17.00
Five Pounds	£5	£5	£80.95
Ten Pounds	£10	£10	£161.89

CARTOONS

"That was delicious—my compliments to the chef."

"Thank you, M'sieu."

LAUGHTER

"Will you listen? I'm an atheist, I tell you!"

"Well, Smedley—did you have a pleasant weekend and forty-five minutes?"

"He tried everything! Chocolates, soft lights, sweet music . . . and they all worked."

ANDY CAPP

YER GETTIN' T'BE QUITE A REGULAR IN THIS OLD PLACE, MISS

I LOVE ANCIENT BUILDINGS, THE LINK WITH THE PAST AND ALL THAT—

MMM... VERY TASTY

SO YER LIKE OLD RUINS—?

AS LONG AS THEY DON'T PESTER ME WHILE I'M TALKING TO SOMEBODY ELSE!

Printed in Great Britain
by Amazon